on
the
edge
of
rain

on
the
edge
of
rain

Dave Ward

H

HEADLAND

First published in 2009
by
HEADLAND PUBLICATIONS
38 York Avenue
West Kirby, Wirral
CH48 3JF

British Library Cataloguing in Publication Data.
A full CIP record for this book is available from the British Library
ISBN: 978 1 902096 56 8

*Front cover and internal images
by Jennifer Firkins © 2009.*

*Back cover image by
Leila Romaya and Paul McCann © 2009.*

Printed in Great Britain by
Oriel Studios, Orrell Mount
Hawthorne Road
Merseyside L20 6NS

HEADLAND acknowledges the financial
assistance of Arts Council England.

CONTENTS

INTRODUCTION

Soulful, sensual and tender, Dave Ward's poems combine a precise use of language with a vivid cinematic imagination. Always there is compassion and empathy and sense that the self is reliant upon others, part of something bigger than itself, be this a feeling of community or the energies of the natural world.

Often Dave Ward presents poetic fragments to the reader, not for interpretation or analysis but as things in themselves with the same properties and values as a leaf or a blade of grass. They are natural occurrences with meanings that cannot be reduced to simple descriptions or logical explanations but have to be experienced within the imagination.

The poet often disappears into the poem, into the rhythm and silence that surrounds the words. Sometimes this is beautiful, delicate and strong; sometimes it is nightmarish, painful and disturbing. Different shades of imagination are rendered in lucid close-up. In these poems imagination is an experience, not an abstraction but a felt reality, a dream and a vision.

ELEANOR REES

WHERE THE WORLD BEGINS

Where The World Begins was commissioned by Taiwanese film-maker Chen Chieh-jen as part of his proposal to Tate Liverpool for Liverpool Biennial 2006.

An audio version of the poem, performed with Eleanor Rees and Curtis Watt with music and production by Ade Jackson, was installed alongside Chen Chieh-jen's film *The Route*.

A live performance version took place in Tate Liverpool on 29th October 2006.

A pamphlet version was made available to visitors to the exhibition.

'Though your dreams be tossed and blown...'
from *You'll Never Walk Alone*: Rodgers and Hammerstein.

'Neptune was the last to go...'
from *Big River*: Jimmy Nail.

Thanks to Kevin Robinson for insight and information on Liverpool Docks and the Dockers' dispute.

In memory of Sandy, who sold the *Liverpool Echo* for many years at Liverpool's Pier Head.

Thanks to Eleanor Rees for editorial advice, encouragement and support.

WHERE THE WORLD BEGINS

This is where the world begins.
This is where the river ends.

The sea beyond the sea.
The sea beneath the sea.

The city's dark manacles hold us here,
the sailors who never put to sea,
delving out treasure
from the depths of sunless holds.

Dock walls like fortresses
hoarding the grain,
hoarding the sugar,
hoarding the pain.

Smell of diesel,
smell of sea,
smell of burgers,
coffee and grease.

Suck of the estuary,
suck of the sea,
suck of the city inside.

*

Containers stacked, rusting and cracked,
packed with fertiliser, fish meal and grain.

Branded with codes of old journeys, old dockets,
old cargoes, old routes, old shipping lines.

Rain-lashed and haggard, stubborn and battered,
groaning from dockside to port.

Cobwebs and dust corroded by salt,
sick wind hangs dumb in dark spaces between.

*

In front of the glowering Liver Buildings,
    under the bus-shelter's friendless shadow,
        under the eye of the Liver Birds,
    the skyline which does not sleep:
    the gateway to the river, to the world,
        to Birkenhead -

Sandy limps like a scurrying crab across flagstones
flecked with chewing-gum.

Sandy sells the Echo
and collects cups stained with maps of tea
to take back to the all-night café.

A hatch in the wall at the old Pier Head
where he can watch the river wash up against the wall.

        An eye on the river.
        An eye on the world.

His voice is blind and broken.

Late revelers come and talk to him
and bring him drink, and buy him chips.

*

The night's silence wraps her arms
   around the big machines;
cradles their roar to a whisper,
   their trundling anger tugged gently away,
washed out to sea on the wind.

The wind blows the other way
   all through the day;
swirls the curses, the banter, the jibes,
   the clattering racket of the high straddle carriers,
the swoop and plunge of the cranes.

But at night they glide,
   grey ghosts in the darkness,
sudden shadows creeping over and above,
   behind, beside...

   Silence of moonlight,
     silence of rooftops,
      silence of water
        lapping dark below.

   Listen...
     Listen...
      Listen...

*

Sandy's cry of 'Echo' echoes:
'Echchchooooo...'
mournful as a fog-horn on a dark winter night.

The ferry butting against the landing stage.
The heavy rattle of chains.

This is the sea, here in the river,
this is the tide which tugs.

The city's flotsam
floating down to the water
to hang around the Pier Head
under the shadows of the Liver Buildings.

Winos and land-locked sailors sit here
entranced on empty benches;
grandfathers gazing rheumy-eyed
out towards the sea,
while grandchildren, little ones,
play on the grass between the benches -
oblivious to it all.

Snarling seabirds mimic the voices
of families trapped on hard metal benches
scrapping over a bag of cold chips,
up-turned ice-cream cones trickling in the dust,
the coffee hot in heavy mugs.

Cold wind blows the litter
and take-away wrappers,
and they just want to go home.

*

Sandy sees it all,
boarding the buses when the drivers wave him on:
riding down Dale Street and out through the town...
Everton Brow and Fazackerley...
anywhere he wants for free.
Pitching and tossing through shimmering traffic -
out to the terminus and all the way back.

*

The bow of the boat moves slowly
through slow moving slow grey water.

Each day longer than a day,
lost on an endless journey.

Nothing but the throb of the engines.
Nothing but the wheel of the sky.

Rattle of laughter echoes forgotten.
Watching long shadows cast over the side.

*

Sandy wakes each morning
to the croak of the buses' exhaust fumes,
the clatter of office clerks' feet
and the clank of the ferry boats pulling off.

Dawnlight rising,
a skirl of gulls,
flapping litter and lost-eyed girls.

Lost souls swirling home.
Lost voices in the wind.

    'Though your dreams be tossed and blown...'

The cough of fog, a wracking sound,
the rattle of huge chains running down.

*

In the streets that their fathers trudged,
dockers' kids play hopscotch now -
pitch and toss and kick the ball.

Robbie Fowler (Some call him God)
displays his T-shirt to the Kop:
'SUPPORT THE LIVERPOOL DOCKERS'
emblazoned across his chest.

'Nothing falls up',
the old hands said.
'Keep looking to the sky,
keep your hat on your head.'

'Men with thirty years of service,
men engrained in company loyalty,
men who know nothing but life on the docks -
cast out to stand on the picket line.'

Feeding the five hundred:
for every man a family -
feeding the five thousand,
a rattle of coins chucked into collection buckets
every Saturday afternoon.

*

The Women of the Waterfront,
daughters, wives and mothers,
dancing on the pavement
outside the bosses' houses;
their voices raised together
to shame Scabs to their neighbours;
singing all the latest hits,
    'Neptune was the last to go,
      I heard it on my radio' -
lighting candles, swaying arms,
to a raucous ghetto-blaster.

People who've never seen each other
meet up through the dispute -
all along the waterfront
and every corner of the docks:

'Coming together like a giant pan of Scouse.'

*

Sad-eyed Sandy leaps up and down,
his raincoat flapping forlorn as a clown,
while a straggle of children stand around
watching the bag beneath him writhe,
shackled in chains and triple-tied,
till with one mighty bound the man inside
breaks free and bows like an acrobat -
and Sandy passes round the hat.

*

The cranes along the sky-line,
a slow dance in unison.

Sunset fills the silences,
dipping low and beckoning,
trapped in glints which sit on the windowsills
of the terraced rows in Birkenhead.

*

Sandy stands where the sea meets the river,
the river meets the land:
where these worlds merge - a no-man's land.

    Sandy is no-man.
    Sandy is everyone.

Sandy drifts dreaming on the Seventy-Two
down the tree-lined mile of Menlove Avenue,
riding out to the Priory
to collect his crust of bread
and his cup of luke-warm soup.

Then on to the turn-around at the Horses Rest,
beside gap-toothed headstones for long-lost pets,
cadging bacon and burgers
at the trailer in the lay-by.

This is where the sky begins.
This is where the city ends.
    But Sandy turns back -
back to the streets that taste of the sea.

    Old shopping precincts peel and decay,
    clapboard faces flaking,
    weatherworn and weary
        as mothers in headscarves
    tugging their kids, frantic in the wind.

Lost ghosts throng and wave
behind the high metal railings
of the gaunt nursing home on the corner,
calling and singing through tall grey trees,
hiding behind the dull shadows of leaves
where derelict summer-houses slither and rot.

    The Jewish cemetery at Springwood.
    White gravestones picked out in neat rows
    behind the black-chained fence.

Blundering back to the old drinking clubs:
Dutch Eddies, the Embassy, Gladray and Tun-Tum
pulsing all-night reggae rhythms
seeping into the veins of traffic
surging down Upper Parliament Street.

    The late-night Somali café.
    Silhouettes of old sailors sit
        hunched over dominoes
    in the window.

Shadows of Chinatown's Sunday morning market,
squawk of cockerels trapped in baskets.
Tall men in robes and pigtails
haunt the Nelson Street doorways.

By the side of the dusty dock road
an old woman in a purple coat
and make-up pale as the moon
presses against the bars of the fence,
clips strands of lavender straggling wild
and tucks them into her brown leather bag.

      Time travels.
      Time trawls.

Sandy sees it all.
Sees everything.
Sees nothing -
only the next unsold Echo, the empty cups of tea.

Sad and bedraggled, Sandy watches.
His coat hangs dull, the colour of dust.
Never sleeping, never waking.
He is always here.
    Listen...
        Listen...
            Listen...

*

A ragged straggle of coppers,
sick to the back teeth
of getting dragged down to the picket line again -
standing around in the biting cold
waiting for something to happen,
while the dockers huddle together
sizzling sausages on the brazier,
fetching mugs of steaming tea
from the caravan at Seaforth Gate.

*

Sandy stumbles like the Pier Head pigeons:
living just under the horizon's rim, but never seeing
the sea.
Land-bound, a hobbled strut, head jerking back and forth;
always on the look-out for left-overs,
scratting.

Time slips
   ships in a bottle
   sliding from hand to lips.

The cargoes come and go but still the river flows,
pitching outward, lee and yaw,
furrowing the field of the sea
where white gulls swoop and swirl,
following the plough of tankers and freighters.

Night star, dawn star. Dog Star. Dog Watch.

Sandy stands in a place where there is sand no more.
Tarmac and concrete replace the sandflats, the ripples,
the sandbanks, the dunes.

This city pours through the narrow funnel
of the landing stage jetty into the ferry.

Traffic of feet
    of shoppers
    of sailors
    of dockers
    of slaves.

Dawn becomes morning, becomes day, slopes into
afternoon.

Listen...
    Listen...
        Listen...

*

At Seaforth, Gladstone, Hornby, Canada,
the pickets move slowly, shuffling on the line;
dry mouths, cold hands and heavy limbs -
waiting for the word for a lightning mass protest
outside a different gate.

Dry mouths, cold hands and heavy limbs.
Muted in the sullen mist that rolls in from the sea.
Waiting for the O.S.D. to skid snarling into view,
brandishing black batons from the backs of open
landrovers.

'Don't take them on, lads.'
Waiting till their tyres judder to a halt
before quickly stepping aside.

Eyes staring, not seeing.
Seeing all, seeing nothing.
Dry mouths, cold hands and heavy limbs.

Chaos in the city as traffic backs-up, rerouted
and buses filled with extra police trundle down to the docks.
The O.S.D. watching, chewing gum
fingers twitching,
waiting while the regulars flounder into flack-jackets
before they drive away.

Police lines, picket lines, watching and waiting.
Dry mouths, cold hands and heavy limbs.

'Okay lads, that's it. Let's go.'

And the dockers fade away, into the mist,
into the morning,
leaving the police just standing,
frustrated at the gate.

*

Sandy hears the dockers' voices,
sees the ghosts of long-gone sailors,
always present by their absence.
    never at home, at home.
Hears the clatter of passengers
    down the slipway, onto the landing stage
    from the days when the ferries were full.

He sees them in his dreams.
They are his dreams.

Selling the Echo he never reads,
the pockets of his rain-soaked mac
hang grubby with loose change.

*

Dull sun glints on the optics
behind the bar at the Elm House pub.

By the window a gang of dockers sits huddled,
debating moves and strategies
over endless mugs of morning tea.

Dust settles on their gear stowed in the corner
before they swing out to the picket line
up the road at Seaforth gate.

As the door closes behind them
an unread newspaper slithers to the floor.

'Don't believe what you read in the Echo.'

*

A city lit by stars
glistening across cold rooftops.
While she sleeps,
a fist comes knocking at the door.

Listen...
    Listen...
        Listen...

    The sea beneath the sea.
    The sea beyond the sea.

This is where the world begins.
This is where the river ends.

ON THE EDGE OF RAIN

is a diary of poems for Eleanor Rees.
The form fell naturally into place from the first poem
onwards and became a daily journal to chronicle journeys,
memories and shared experiences.

Sections have appeared in *Neon Highway*
and *The Binturog Review* .

*

in this heat
white flowers wander

shadows hang languid
behind silent door

red petals strewn
across morning floor

*

touch this leaf
flesh of tree

brush shimmering skin
a trembling body

kiss flowing sap
hold the energy

*

cloud dancing down
to dark rivers

winding deep between
thrust of hills

trance of silence
soft breathing still

*

at river's turning
beat of wing

long fields slope
past summer's wind

old bracken burns
where skylarks sing

*

let darkness out
breathe softness in

light shadows dance
stairs of rain

birds voices twist
shrill and keening

*

sunshine and smoke
drift shadowing eyes

awake in dream
day enters slow

slope of silence
across spiraling sky

*

bruise of moon
an aching tug

dark trees gather
shadows of love

pale limbs dance
while strangers pass

*

under beckoning dusk
scream sudden wings

beat of feathers
pulse of bone

dark air panic
still waters run

*

red leaves falling
slip the wind

skirt of stardust
hands of rain

call music's laughter
from silent rooms

*

ghost violin plays
in the wind

at the end
of the field

a girl sits
the path begins

*

milk white moon
spills autumn seed

across the river
dark boats lure

ghost streets run
with scarlet leaves

*

veins of sap
lace waiting trees

pale pavements leaf
bright scattered stones

street of birds
skirl caged windows

*

bird's wing map
spread in flight

grey of sea
grey of sky

over the horizon
another horizon calls

*

a silver morning
petals fly purple

slow circles turn
the leaving season

frail bones lattice
across cobwebbed field

*

rain leaves rattle
pale voices touch

sky shivers frail
flower mouths moist

snow fires beckon
caressing warm breath

*

edge of light
far fields calling

scarred hands healing
the river's night

circle of journeys
turning in flight

BRUSHSTROKES OF BREATH

These poems were informed and inspired by the practice of Qi Gong and readings of the Tao as well as my visit to Singapore as Writer in Residence at Nan Yang University in 1999.

A selection, including original art-work by Xia Lu, was produced in a hand-made limited edition by Mairie Gelling/*Word in the Hand* for my visit to China, funded by Arts Council England in 2006.

The poems formed the basis for readings, workshops, seminars and discussions at schools in Hong Kong and at Heilongjiang University and Harbin Normal University.

*

take an empty cup
    make sure it is clean

fill the cup with water
    be sure the water is pure

place a pebble in the cup full of water
    choose one carefully - shining and smooth

when the pebble sinks to the bottom of the cup
water will spill out over the top

collect this water in a bowl
    make sure the bowl is clean

drink the water from the bowl

in this water taste the pebble
    which still lies in the cup

taste its texture

taste the sunshine which warmed it
    on the hillside where it lay

taste the wind which honed it

taste the silence of the mountain
    which still breathes at its core

*

brushstrokes of cloud
across a breathing sky

*

a tapestry of silence
dreams through silver night

*

beside the shining bridge
lanterns of darkness glow

*

inside its stone-brown shell
the snail carries dreams of flying

*

the skull of the moth
is filled with dark light

*

in the bone forest
stone flowers slowly grow

*

behind a blue door a father watches
his daughter's singing sky

*

when the mirror swings from side to side
the reflection's eye hangs still

*

tracks of highwire thistledown
scar the circus field

*

from beyond unending nebulae
the seeds of planets ride

*

a celandine seeks its own shadow
at noon

*

at dusk
the seeds of voices fall

*

every road out of town
winds slowly home

*

even slow grey snails
go trailing bright colours

*

the light's desire is to fly
to the wings of the beckoning moth

*

when the mountain-top feels close to touch
it is further than the sky

*

the pen is a stem of breath
tipped with waking wonder

*

at the centre of silence
beats the stillness of sound

*

some nights
it is the dance
that leads to the dream

some nights
it is the dream
that leads to the dance

some nights
to dream the dream
is all we need

some nights
to dance the dance
is enough

*

If the blossom petal touches your shoulder,
turn and smile.

If the blossom petal touches your cheek,
gently blush.

If the blossom petal touches your lips,
kiss the wind.

*

For your happiness:

Bathe your face with trembling birdsong
    stolen from a moonlit meadow.

Open your window at daybreak's touch
    and let the dew taste your skin.

Caress the music of memories
    locked in a yellowing leaf.

Listen to the colours of the river
    drifting in the evening wind.

Dance down dreaming avenues
    while the blossom's soft breath
        follows you.

*

I cannot see you

but I see you.

I cannot hear you

but I hear you.

Where are you?

You are with me.

I can touch you.

Reach for me.

*

how can I remember you?

remember smile
        as warm as wind
remember hands
        as soft as dew
remember eyes
        as deep as moon

how can I remember you?

I cannot see your blushing smile
I cannot touch your singing hands
I cannot feel your fluttering eyes
watching me
        as I watched you

how can I remember you?

but wind is in the swaying trees
dew is damp on glistening grass
moon stares down from silver clouds

they are here

and so are you

*

mountain is grey sky
sky is grey mountain

lost in pale rain
following cloudsong

wait for the journey
the journey is waiting

mountain is grey sky
sky is grey mountain

*

I carry this vessel of water
to give to you without spilling.

I cross stony ground.
I claw round sharp thorns.

I carry this vessel of water
under the white silent sun.

Across stony ground
I walk on and on
to bring you this vessel of water,
to give to you without spilling.

When I meet you, will you be thirsty?
Will you take the vessel I have brought
without ever spilling one drop?

Will you have water to give in exchange
at the end of this burning journey?

Will you offer your vessel
and will you take mine,
from hand to hand, from hand to mouth
without ever spilling one drop?

Now that I come to you
at the end of this journey -
are you still thirsty?

Will you drink this water with me?

*

fold the cloth once
it will warm you

fold the cloth twice
it will wrap you in its arms

fold the cloth again
it will smother you

keep folding the cloth
it will cover the moon, the sky

*

Make your hands a cup.

Fill your hands with water:
the water runs through your fingers.

Fill your hands with sand:
the sand trickles slowly away.

Fill your hands with clay:
your fingers mould the oozing mud
slowly into the shape
of everything you desire.

Hold a stone in your hands:
cradle it all day,
until its cold rough surface
yields with glowing warmth.

Fill your hands with air:
your fingers touch the sky;
you can feel the universe
breathing through your palms.

*

this journey
is longer
than a blackbird's song

this journey
is sweeter
than the nectar of the wind

this journey
is harsher
than a broken storm

this journey
turns circles -
at the end is the beginning
at the beginning is the end

*

This dream is a dream of the dream. Shallow shadows. The shadows dance. Across the stream. Across the surface. We can touch the air.

Can we ever touch the dream?

*

How far have we come? To a bridge. The same bridge we cross every day. To go back we have to go forward. To go forward we have to go back. Time hangs. At this bridge it is the same time now as it has always been.

*

what was here
is still here

what will be here
is here now

TIGER DEW

These pieces are based on an idea from Qi Gong teacher Xia Lu, exploring the five Chinese elements of metal, water, wood, earth and fire.

Sections have been published in *Slacker Sounds* and performed at the Ikonography Gallery, Mathew Street, Liverpool, for the opening of the exhibition *Fire and Eurhythmy*, curated by Nicole Bartos.

*

In the sky is blue distance. Azure, topaz. Tiger Dew
breathes colours. The colours become her. She is the sky.
The sky is her. Inside her, beyond her.

She flies. Without movement. As far as she sees, she is.
There are no boundaries, no walls. Her breath is the
breath of sun, breath of starlight, breath of moons.

The planets turn within her. She is axis, she is orbit. They
turn the tides of her body, but her body is gone. Is one
breath with the breathing, one energy.

One motion is one mile is one thousand miles, is inside
her. She travels through herself to know herself. Her
eyes are galaxies.

She knows everything, sees everything.
Knows nothing at all.

*

She stands at the river bank and raises her arms. Her
robe only hides the robe of her body. Her body is a robe
of skin. Of flesh, of sinews. Of desire, of wanting.

She wants to cast it off. To fly truly naked with the birds.
Swooping and dipping above the skin of the water.
Climbing and diving through the tides of the sky.

But the birds' tawny plumage is also a robe that hides
their true nature. Each an element within a mesh of
elements. All intermingle. All fused.

All one.

*

She lies in the wood. Her skin is snow. Slowly tracks appear. The spoor of creatures: wolf, fox, goose. The fingerprints of lovers.

Tiger Dew smiles. She is kissing sky. She is kissing moon. She strokes her belly and closes her eyes. Touches herself between her thighs. She shivers gently. A distant vixen cries.

Darkness shrouds a robe around her nakedness. Tiger Dew looks up. The moon has gone.

*

In the tree, the hanging man sings slowly to himself as he swings from side to side. A low groan. The song is old, dredged from the depths of his throat.

As the last notes drift lingering into the air, the hanging man springs deftly up onto the bough. Shakes the noose from his neck and scrambles through the branches, agile and lithe.

He clambers down, and as his feet touch the ground, he scampers away light-footed through the rustling leaves. Behind him, the noose dangles darkly from the tree.

*

In a half-lit café at the end of a derelict street, a girl is dancing on a small raised stage.

The café is empty. The tables heavy with dust and silence. Shadows come and go, to sit hunched over one cup of coffee, a slow cigarette. Pages from old newspapers slither to the floor.

The girl dances on, her hair tied back in a dun-coloured scarf, her pleated skirt swaying casually. She dances as if she is waiting for a lover she has never met, but no-one ever comes.

The occasional customers take no notice of her.
The pot-bellied man behind the bar mops the floor and wipes the top of the counter, but always the dust returns, spinning in the spectral light beside the curtained stage.

He runs a hand across his balding head and rubs his greasy hair. Tugs at his braces and starts to whistle.

As he whistles he gazes across at the stage. The girl is dancing faster now, her pale lips twisting into a smile.

The man busies himself, polishing glasses, stacking plates, emptying tarnished ashtrays into the depths of a grimy bin.

He whistles faster as he works and the girl dances quicker too, clapping her hands and clicking her heels in a flurry of rhythm.

The man locks and bolts the door, closes the blinds. He has stopped whistling now. He takes a broom and slowly sweeps the empty stage.

There is no-one there at all.

*

A boy sits in the doorway of a boarded-up shop. His hands are on fire. His limbs are shaking. His eyes bright with anguish. His hands are on fire but he is not consumed. He does not burn.

In the entrance of the next shop an old woman squats.

Her back is arched. She is screaming, hands gripping at the handle of the door behind her. She is giving birth. She gives birth to a tree. The branches, the leaves and then the thick trunk, slithering from her vulva.

She gives one last push and the roots emerge, and then the tree lies before her, bloodied and trembling. The old woman hitches her stockings and sits up. The tree gives a cry.

*

Each morning when she wakes, Rain Girl reaches out to touch the trinkets which lie by her bed. The bracelets, the brooches, the ear-rings, the pendants. Without them she cannot be the person she wishes to be. She rises slowly and stands before the mirror, sliding the baubles onto her wrists, her arms, her ears, her neck.

She runs her fingers through the ringlets of her hair. Smiling, she becomes herself. She slips into her dress.

As she moves through the room she passes through the shadows of every movement she made the night before. The day before. The weeks and months before.

She passes through the shadows of her emotions, her moods, her ecstasy and tears. She passes through her dreams, her memories, her forgetting.

They cling to her like cobwebs, like gossamer, which she can feel, can touch, but in the slow waking dawn she is not sure what they are. Are reflections, are dust. Are nothing at all.

Are fused with the half-glimpsed refractions of all the others who have ever lived in this room. Have visited even briefly. Have only passed through.

They touch Rain Girl's shoulder. They press against her thighs. They brush up against her breasts.

Rain Girl returns to the mirror and rubs a hurried kiss of lipstick across her hungry mouth. She unfurls the spokes of a broken umbrella, a skeleton of wire hung with tattered rags.

She pulls on a coat and opens the door. Outside it is morning. A fine rain is falling.

*

Rain Girl slopes through hissing drizzle. She is stealing whispers, stealing tears. Stealing loose change from the pockets of strangers. Waiting for rainbows in cold damp doorways.

A thin figure joins her. He is hunched inside a long dull coat. His face is pinched and squinny. He peers at Rain Girl. She stares beyond him, watching sheets of water wrapping the shop fronts, hugging lamp-posts.
He asks her for a light.

Rain Girl turns. Her eyes are sparking. She reaches inside her jacket pocket and pulls out a string of lighters on a tarnished silver chain.

The man leans in close to her. His breath smells like a dog. His face is thin and weary. His eyes dull and silent. He balances a loosely-rolled cigarette between pale thin lips.

Rain Girl thrums a lighter. Nothing happens. She tries another one. Tries again. Finally the last one ignites.

The man cradles his hand around the flickering flame. Rain Girl can feel his body shaking. Can read his ribs, count his bones.

He slips an arm around her waist. Tries to kiss her. Rain Girl turns away. Shoves a hand inside his pants and pulls him close. Suddenly.

The man moans and shivers. Shuts his eyes. Takes one more drag on his drooping fag-end then slumps away. Dissolves into the mist of the drizzling street.

Rain Girl hauls the string of lighters back into her jacket. With her other hand she flicks open the man's bedraggled wallet. She eyes it slowly. Expects to find nothing. It's only a habit...

*

Rain Girl twists the frames of supermarket trolleys. She unpicks their mesh, moulds them and shapes them, twining the spiraling wires.

In the back yard she piles them. Crooked crows sculpted from thin brittle metal. Cowering cats, spindled gibbets.

One she shapes like herself. Hangs it with trinkets rattling darkly with rust. Drapes her coat around its shoulders to keep it warm at night.

And in the darkness the rats come and piss on it as they scrabble through its aching frame. The thin wind strips its veins and moonlight wraps cold fingers around every link, every chain.

But in the silence of the morning, Rain Girl leans against the bin, sipping strong tea and watching the effigy.

Listens to it as it moans, as it rattles, as it creaks. Listens to it stutter.

Listens to it speak.

WHERE THE WHITE WIND BLOWS

These three poems have been recorded with Ric Ash as songs, chants and celebrations for the CD *The Green Man Dances.*

Willow Woman appears in *The Doghouse Book of Ballads.*

ONE BOY STOOD IN THE FIELD

One boy stood in the field alone
The wind blows over
The wind blows back
Nothing grows where the white wind blows
One boy stood in the field

Two boys side by side in the field
The wind blows over
The wind blows back
Nothing grows where the white wind blows
Two boys stood in the field

Three boys planted the field with corn
The wind blows over
The wind blows back
Green shoots grew where the white wind blew
Three boys stood in the field

Four boys pulled the weeds and thorns
The wind blows over
The wind blows back
Tall corn grew where the white wind blew
Four boys stood in the field

A score of boys reaped the golden corn
The wind blows over
The wind blows back
Stacked it up in long straight rows
A score of boys in the field

A hundred millers milled the grain
The wind blows over
The wind blows back
Stored in barns from the cold and rain

A hundred milled the grain
A thousand bakers baked the bread
The wind blows over
The wind blows back
Cooked in ovens glowing red
A thousand baked the bread

The boy in the field was not alone
The wind blows over
The wind blows back
A million people ate the loaves
A million people fed

The boy in the field was not alone
The wind blows over
But it won't blow back
The boy in the field was not alone
One boy stood in the field

WILLOW WOMAN

In the tall tower
    a woman is weaving -
In the tall tower
    without window or door.

    What does she weave with,
        this willowing woman? -
    She weaves with silk threads
        wound into a ball.

What does she weave with,
    this willowing woman -
In the tall tower
    without window or door?

    What does she weave with,
        this willowing woman,
    When she has no silk thread
        to weave any more?

When the silk thread is gone,
    this willowing woman
Weaves on with feathers,
    with cobwebs, with straw.

    When the straw turns to dust
        in her hurrying fingers,
    How will she weave
        in the tower with no door?

She weaves with her own hair,
    this willowing woman,
She weaves with her own hair
    which flows down to the floor.

When her hair is all twined,
   this willowing woman -
What does she weave with
   when her hair has all gone?

She weaves with her dreams,
   with her wishes, her secrets -
She weaves with the birdsong
   which streams through the walls.

She weaves night and day,
   this willowing woman -
For she cannot leave
   the tall tower at all.

What has she woven,
   this willowing woman -
What has she woven
   in the tower with no door?

She has woven the face
   of her wandering daughter,
Who left in the spring time
   and will come back no more.

In the tall tower
   a woman is weaving -
In the tall tower
   without window or door.

TO THE EARTH

Lay me out beneath the rainclouds
Let my eyes drink in the sky
Leave me here in these high mountains
Where the dark birds wheel and fly

Let the lightning snake my sinews
Let the cold stones pierce my veins
Let the sun gouge out my hunger
Till the shadows steal my pain

Only the whisper of wind will feed me
Only the touch of dew on my face
Only the chains of moonlight will free me
Only the silence of dawn on my breath

Let the roots thread through my fingers
Let the earth embrace my bones
Let my tongue taste webs of starfrost
Leave me here, but not alone

Let my tears run into rivers
Let me feel the forest's cry
Let new life rise through my body
Till at my death, I cannot die

Also by Dave Ward:

FACES Streetword Press 1973
ELECTRIC LOVE Straight Enterprises 1974
GYPSY Moonshine Press 1974
SOMETHING LIKE A SYMPHONY Share 1975
UNCLE STRANGE Moonshine Press 1976
STREET Excello & Bollard 1976
TUFF STUFF Speed Limit 1977
YESTERDAY'S LOVING Aquila 1977
WITH LOVE FROM LIVERPOOL Great Georges 1977
ANGEL VEINS Speed Limit 1977
CEREMONIES/RITUALS Excello & Bollard 1977
WHEN THE SLOW RAIN COMES Toulouse Press 1979
JAMBO Riot Stories Ltd 1982
A GREY VOICE STAINED WITH DREAMS Other 1983
STEREO SOUNDTRACK Stride 1984
THE CIRCUS IN THE SQUARE M.P.M.S. 1984
SMOKY CITY GIRL Bogg USA 1985
BRAILLE Jonathon Press 1989
BLUES FOR JOHNNIE RHYTHM Other 1990
TREE Spike 1993
JAMBO Impact Books 1993
CANDY AND JAZZZ Oxford University Press 1994
TRACTS Headland 1996
THE TREE OF DREAMS HarperCollins 1996
BRUSHSTROKES OF BREATH Word in the Hand 2006
WHERE THE WORLD BEGINS Liverpool Biennial 2006